I0426383

Preliminary Assessment of Diamondback Terrapins *(Malaclemys terrapin)* Nesting Ecology at Sandy Hook, NJ, Gateway National Recreation Area: July – September 2002

Technical Report NPS/NER/NRTR—2005/014

Sylwia E. Ner, M.S. and Dr. Russell. L. Burke

Department of Biology
Hofstra University,
Hempstead, NY 11549

February 2005

U.S. Department of the Interior
National Park Service
Northeast Region
Inventory & Monitoring Program
Boston, Massachusetts

This report was accomplished under Cooperative Agreement 4520-98-017, with assistance from the NPS. The statements, findings, conclusions, recommendations, and data in this report are solely those of the author(s), and do not necessarily reflect the views of the U.S. Department of the Interior, National Park Service.

Please cite this publication as:

Ner, S. E., R. L. Burke. February 2005. Preliminary Assessment of Diamondback Terrapins *(Malaclemys terrapin)* Nesting Ecology at Sandy Hook, NJ, Gateway National Recreation Area: July – September 2002. Technical Report NPS/NER/NRTR—2005/014. National Park Service. Boston, Massachusetts.

Table of Contents

Tables

Figures

Introduction

The Sandy Hook Unit (SHU) is the only part of the Gateway National Recreation Area (GNRA) located in New Jersey. SHU is a peninsula approximately 680 hectares in size, extending north from coastal New Jersey into the confluence of Raritan Bay, Sandy Hook Bay, Lower New York Bay and the Atlantic Ocean. SHU lies at the northern end of New Jersey's barrier island system. Approximately nineteen kilometers (km) of ocean and bay shoreline ring the peninsula, which varies in width from less than one-tenth km to approximately 1.6 km in the widest part.

The most conspicuous turtle species found at SHU is the Northern diamondback terrapin, a brackish water turtle. Terrapins are one of the most latitudinally wide-ranging turtles of North America, ranging from Cape Cod to the Florida Keys, and as far west as the Gulf Coast of Texas (Conant and Collins 1998). Terrapins are the only turtles in the U.S. that regularly inhabit tidal creeks, bays, coastal marshes, estuaries, and salt marshes, where the salinity ranges from zero to almost full salt water. In the early spring, terrapins come out from hibernation and spend their time feeding and mating. During June, July, and early August, adult females cross the intertidal zone to nest on sandy dunes. Through late summer, terrapins spend most of their time feeding in deep waters in preparation for the winter hibernation (Roosenburg 1991). At this same time, terrapin hatchlings emerge from their nests. Hatchlings emerge from late August through September and early October, while some may overwinter in the nest and emerge the following spring. The diet of *M. terrapin* mainly consists of dead fish, crabs, snails, shrimp, clams and other invertebrates. Terrapins may be an important component of estuarine food webs (Hurd et al. 1979), but more research is needed to determine their role in the ecosystem.

Objectives at Sandy Hook in 2002

a) Estimate the number of terrapins nesting at the SHU in summer of 2002
b) Document the location(s) of the most important SHU terrapin nesting beaches, both in terms of most nests and most hatchlings produced
c) Estimate the average clutch size of terrapins nesting at SHU
d) Estimate the number of clutches laid per year by terrapins at SHU
e) Determine the length of the 2002 terrapin nesting season at SHU
f) Determine the relative amount of terrapins nesting at night vs. nesting in day
g) Estimate the overall predation rate on SHU terrapin nests in 2002
h) Determine which species are important terrapin nest predators at SHU
i) Determine the number of adult terrapins killed by vehicular traffic in 2002
j) Determine the hatching success rate for non-predated SHU terrapin nests in 2002
k) Collect standard morphological data on as many terrapins as possible for comparison to similar data from other GNRA populations
l) Uniquely mark as many terrapins as possible as a basis for future survivorship studies
m) Attach return tags to as many terrapins as possible to gather data on long term movements
n) Collect small blood samples from a sample of SHU terrapins for genetic comparison with other GNRA populations

Methods

During a summer 2001 visit we examined all potential nesting areas that might be used by nesting terrapins (Figure 1). We established that nesting terrapins utilize at least three different areas of the Sandy Hook peninsula: near the old gun batteries (the "Battery Zone", on the eastern portion of the SH), in a sandy area right across from the Seagull's Nest Restaurant (the "Critical Zone"), and in the Holly Forest (Figure 2).

In late May 2002 Sylwia Ner and an assistant began more intensive work at SHU. We made regular surveys along the western shore line from the northern end of Horseshoe Cove to Plum Island. The number of surveys per day varied according to weather conditions and tide (Table 1), beginning on 1 June 2002 and ending 1 August 2002. During sunny weather and at high tides surveys were carried out approximately hourly during daylight hours. An average of 4.3 hours were spent surveying each day (range 0.5 hr – 10 hr), except for 15 June and 30 June when no surveys were done. Surveys entailed walking along the beach, looking for emergent terrapins or their tracks, and similarly examining adjacent nesting areas. The Battery Zone, the Critical Zone, and the Holly Forest sites, identified during the 2001 season, were revisited (Figure 2), and new nesting sites were found by observing the movements of nesting females tracked from their emergence from the ocean. When terrapins were encountered on shore they were observed as inconspicuously as possible until they nested, unless they were either already disturbed or already done nesting. It was easy to identify females that had finished nesting by palpation. In these circumstances they were processed and released in the ocean nearby. Park roads were patrolled at the same time for live, injured, and dead terrapins. In the evenings, the beaches of the selected nesting areas were raked with a leaf rake, leaving a clear set of lines in the sand parallel to the water line. Each morning these trails were checked for terrapin and predator tracks.

Samples of randomly chosen nests were protected from predators, using 24 inch by 24 inch squares of ¼ inch hardware cloth screening buried just below the soil surface, over the nest (Feinberg and Burke 2003). These nests were monitored until hatchling emergence, so that we could collect data on hatching success rate for non-predated nests and to indicate normal time from oviposition to emergence.

All observed nests which were not protected were marked and checked daily for predation either until they were predated or until the end of the nesting season (August or September). After early August nests were checked approximately weekly for signs of hatchling emergence until the onset of cold weather. Nests that had not hatched by the onset of cold weather were excavated. All predated, hatched, and unhatched nests were excavated to determine whether any eggs or hatchlings remained, and to make egg shell counts where possible.

Table 1. Data on female terrapins captured at Sandy Hook Unit in 2001. "Date" refers to capture date, notch refers to the scute which was notched (see Figure 3), and "plastron length" refers to straight-midline plastron length.

Date	Return Tag #	Notch	Scute damage	Abnormalities	Plastron length	comments
6/4	1	G	N/A	Extra (2) on 5 scute	187	Not nesting
	2	O	Damaged LM	N/A	170	Not nesting
6/10	3	A			170	1st of two captures
	4	B			171	
	5	C			170	
	6(106)	D			172	1st of two captures
	7	F		Barnacle on Carapace	174	
6/11	8	H			175	
	9	No Notch	Damaged ABP		182	
	10	I		Missing Right Front Limb	177	1st of two captures
	11	J			190	
6/12	12	No Notch	Damaged AP		182	
	13	K			181	
	14	L			177	
	15	M			170	
6/16	16	N			172	
6/21	17	K8Scute			222	
6/22	18	P		Right Rear Leg Wounded	158	
6/23	19	E		Extra (1) 5th scute	184	
6/24	20	No Notch		Unusual Bright Yellow	166	
	21	AC	N/A	N/A	187	
	22	AB				
6/26	23	AD			168	
	24	CD			176	
	25	CE	6 Right Scute		172	
	26	AE	13 Scutes on RT		196	
	27	BD			184	
	28(128)	AF			178	
	29	BE			182	
	30	AG			192	
6/28	3	A			170	2nd of two captures
	6(106)	D				2nd of two captures
	31	AH		Slipper Shell on Plastron	184	
	32	AI			177	
	33	AJ			185	
	34	AK		Carapace Deformed	174	
	35	AL			174	
	36	AM		Shedding	176	
	37	AN			173	
	38	No Notch	M-Missing		151	1st of two captures
6/29	39	AO			170	
	40	AP			180	
7/1	10	I		Missing Right Front Limb		2nd of two captures

Table 1. Data on female terrapins captured at Sandy Hook Unit in 2001. "Date" refers to capture date, notch refers to the scute which was notched (see Figure 3), and "plastron length" refers to straight-midline plastron length (continued).

Date	Return Tag #	Notch	Scute damage	Abnormalities	Plastron length	comments
7/3	41	BF		Shedding	169	
	42	BG			174	
7/10	38	No Notch	M-Missing		151	2nd of two captures
	43	No Notch		Deformed Plastron	186	
	44	BH		Deformed Carapace	189	
7/11	45	BI			171	
7/12	46	BJ	M-Missing		182	
7/15	47	BK			170	
7/17	48	BL			184	
7/19	49	BM			195	

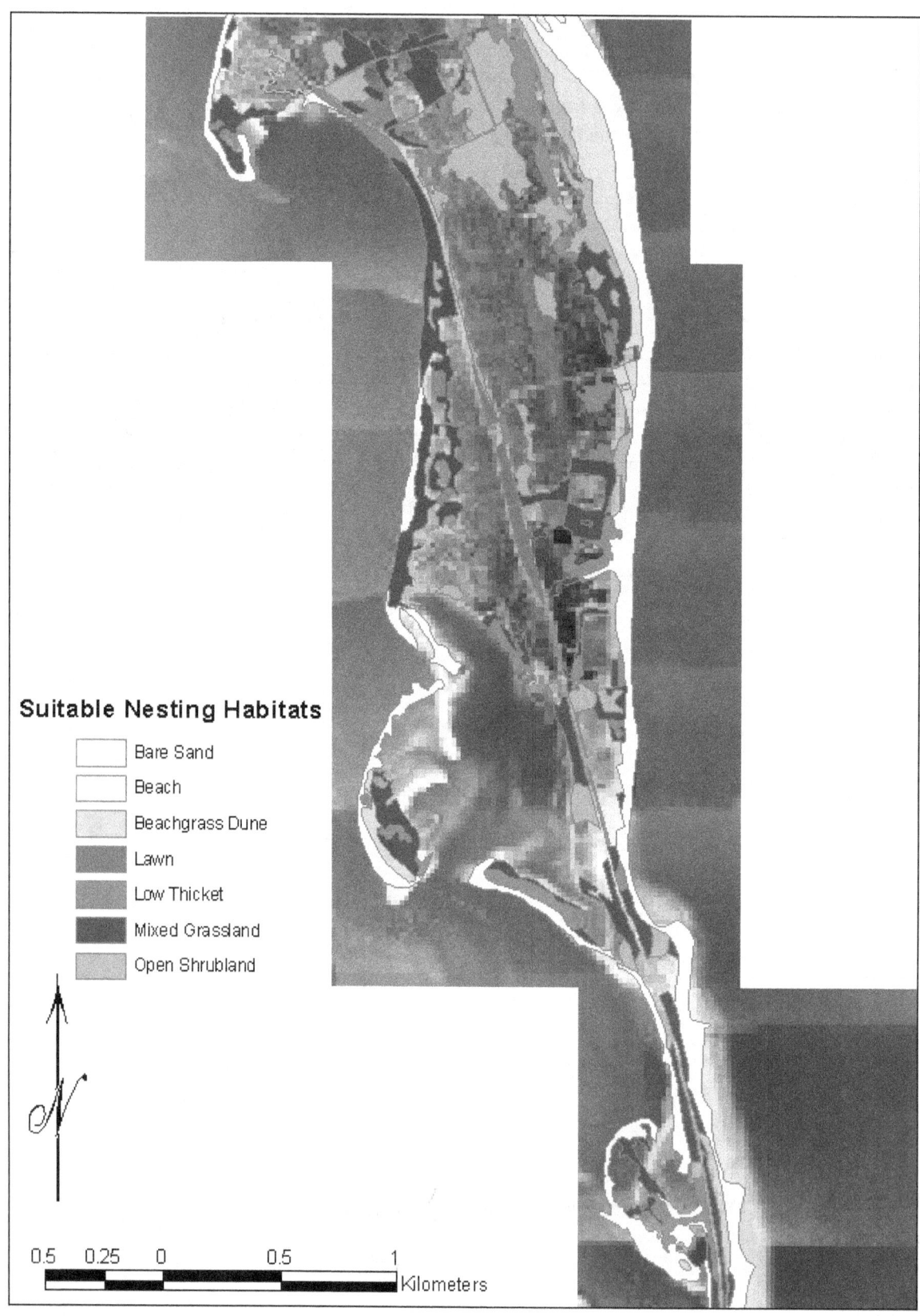

Suitable Nesting Habitats

- Bare Sand
- Beach
- Beachgrass Dune
- Lawn
- Low Thicket
- Mixed Grassland
- Open Shrubland

0.5 0.25 0 0.5 1
Kilometers

Data Source: 1977 aerial photography, 1976 land cover (NPS data)

Figure 1. Location of potential nesting beaches at SHU based on suitable nesting habitats (1997 aerial photography, 1976 land cover data), indicated by different colors, at the Sandy Hook Unit, NJ

8

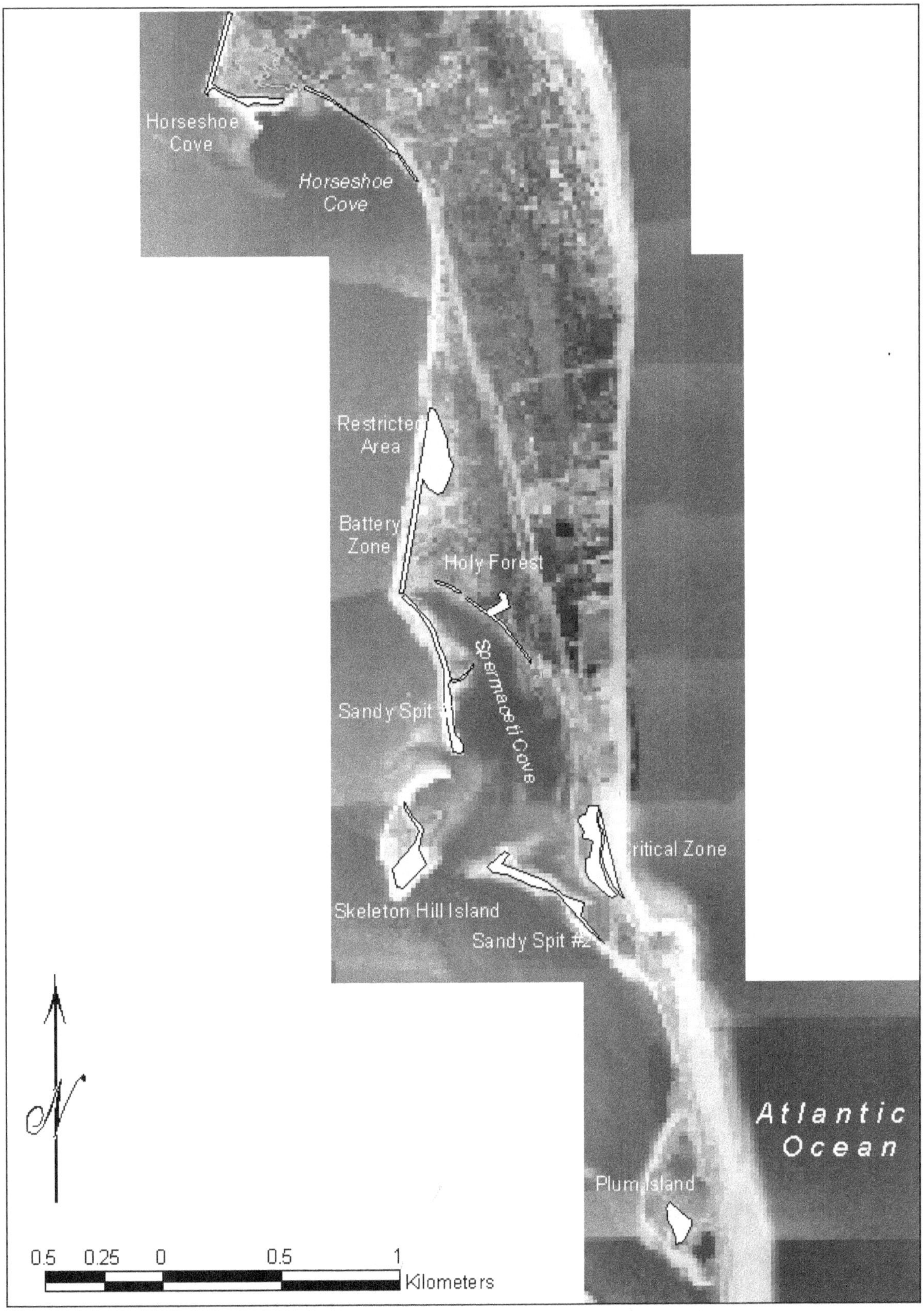

Horseshoe Cove
Horseshoe Cove
Restricted Area
Battery Zone
Holy Forest
Spermaceti Cove
Sandy Spit
Critical Zone
Skeleton Hill Island
Sandy Spit #2
Atlantic Ocean
Plum Island
0.5 0.25 0 0.5 1
Kilometers

Data Source: 1977 aerial photography, 1976 land cover (NPS data)

Figure 2. Location of actual nesting beaches based on 2002 study (1997 aerial photography, 1976 land cover data), indicated by yellow color, at the Sandy Hook Unit, NJ (Produced at Gateway NRA in 2003).

Captured females were measured (Figure 3), inspected for parasites and uniquely notched for future studies of the SHU population (Figure 3). Each female received a unique notch, using a file, so if the female is encountered again multiple clutching could be determined. Metal return tags (Figure 4) were glued with marine epoxy onto the posterior carapace of each adult terrapin. Each tag offered a $10 reward if the tag was returned to a Hofstra University with collection information. Blood samples were taken by snipping off the very tip of tail and blotting a drop of blood on filter paper. Tails were cleaned before and after blood collection using alcohol wipes.

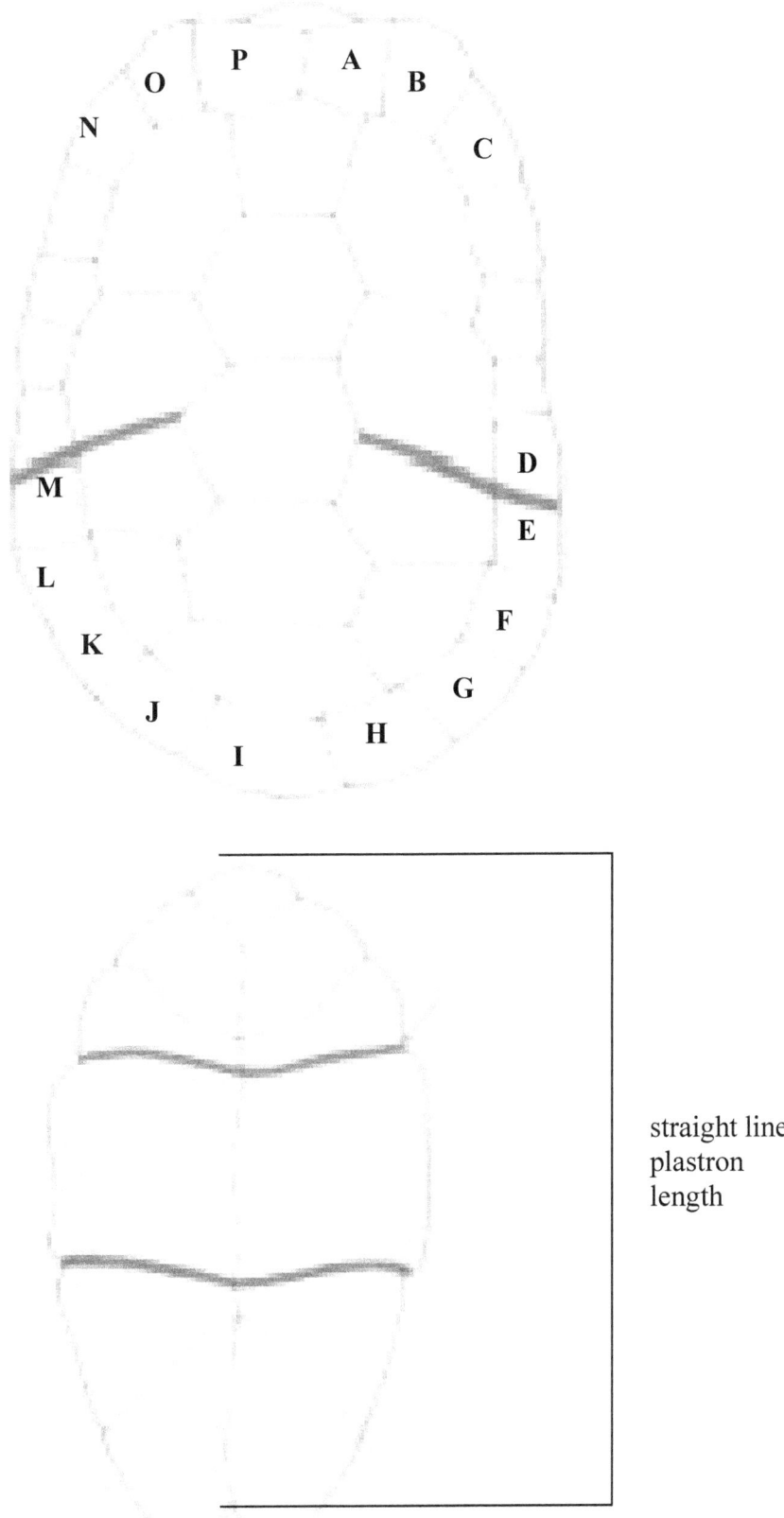

straight line
plastron
length

Figure 3. Terrapin notching system and plastron measuring system.

Figure 4. Front and back of a return tag.

Results

a) The number of terrapin nests at Sandy Hook Unit

Over the course of this study a total of 203 nests were found in SHU. Of these, 170 were predated, we protected 19, and 14 were located post-emergence. During June and July 2002, 49 different turtles were captured and marked at eight different locations of the park (Fig. 2). We frequently observed basking turtles during low tides on Sandy Spit, and at one point we counted approximately 250 females and males. Based on these observations and nests counts we estimate that at a minimum, approximately 200-300 terrapins of both sexes live in Sandy Hook bay.

b) The most important SHU terrapin nesting beaches

We found eight important terrapin nesting areas (Figure 2): Battery Zone, Critical Zone, Holly Forest, Plum Island, Skeleton Hill Island, Horseshoe Cove, Sandy Spit #1 and Sandy Spit; these accounted for 83% of the nesting at SHU (Table 2).

Nesting activity was detected not only by direct observation of nesting females, but also by turtle tracks, predated nests, and post-emergence nesting holes. For example, between late August and the end of September, 14 post-emergence holes were found. Emergence holes contained mostly empty eggshells, undeveloped eggs, and often terrapin hatchlings. Post-emergence holes typically looked like a three cm slit in the ground. Post-emergence holes often had eggshells scattered around the slit in the direction that the hatchlings emerged from the nest.

Table 2. The number of predated nests, nests found by locating emergence holes, and nests we protected, in each of the nesting areas at SH.

Area	Predated Nests	Emergence Hole	Protected Nests	Total
Battery Zone	54	3	3	60
Critical Zone	42	2	1	45
Holly Forest	43	6	15	64
Horseshoe Cove	5	0	0	5
Plum Island	13	3	0	16
Sandy Spit #1	3	0	0	3
Sandy Spit #2	3	0	0	3
Skeleton Hill Island	7	0	0	7
Total	170	14	19	203

c) Estimate the average clutch size of terrapins nesting at SHU

We protected 19 nests using wire mesh excluders. These excluders were successful in keeping raccoons away from the freshly laid nests while incubating. However, clutch size data were obtained from only 11 of these nests, because raccoons predated some of the protected nests after the excluders were removed to ensure safe emergence of hatchlings.

The average clutch size from protected nests was 13.3 ± 3.7 s.d. (n = 11 nests, range 9-19). We also estimated clutch size by examination of the remains inside post-emergence holes, here we found average clutch size to be 9.1 ± 2.80 (n = 14 nests, range 5-13). We also estimated average clutch size by reconstructing eggshell fragments from predated nests, this result was 10.5 ± 3.75 (n = 170 nests, range 3-19). We consider the data from protected nests to be the most accurate. In comparison, the average clutch size for terrapin nests at Jamaica Bay in 2000 and 2001 was 11.8 ± 3.1 s.d. (Giambanco 2003)

d) The number of clutches laid per year by terrapins at SHU

In the absence of either dissected turtles or large field crews, it is impossible to accurately estimate the number of clutches laid per female per year. The number of nests detected does not directly indicate the number of females in the population, because females may lay 0, 1, 2, or 3 clutches during nesting season. In fact, there are no data from any population of terrapins anywhere that can be used to indicate the number of clutches typically laid by females in a year, so the number of clutches laid in an area cannot be used to estimate the number of females in that area.

However we recaptured four nesting females as they returned to nest for a second time (Figure 5). The recaptured females did not return to the same nesting sites, but they did return to the same general location where they first laid nests. There are two weak suggestions that some females may lay three clutches in one season: we caught one female (#38) for the first time, in the middle of the nesting season (on June 28), and again at the end of the nesting season, on 10 July (Figure 5). Two possibilities could explain this pattern. This female might have laid her first clutch while other females were laying their second clutches. Or she might have laid her first clutch at the same time as the other females and we missed her then, and she might therefore have been laying her second clutch on 27th June, and her third on 9 July. If the latter is correct, then this suggests that some females in the SHU population may lay as many as three clutches. Patterns similar to that of #38 have been observed at Jamaica Bay, but again no female has been directly observed laying more than two clutches in a single season. Inspection of Figure 5 also suggests the possibility of a three clutch nesting season (Feinberg and Burke 2003).

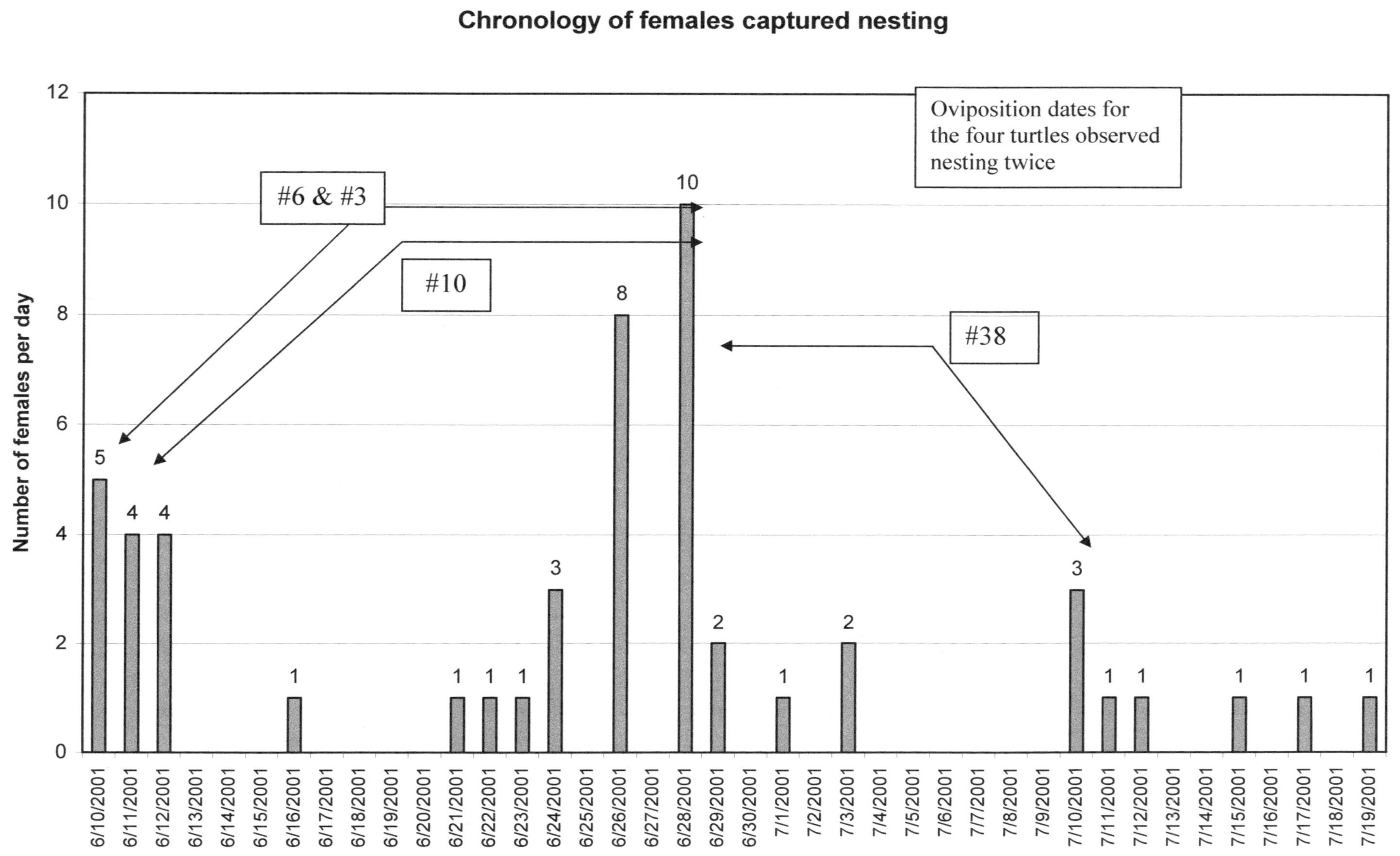

Chronology of females captured nesting

Number of females per day

Figure 5. Chronology of females captured nesting.

#6 & #3

#10

#38

Oviposition dates for the four turtles observed nesting twice

16

e) The length of the 2002 terrapin nesting season at SHU

Although the first female terrapin was not captured until 4 June, we discovered the first indications of nesting (a predated nest) on 1 June and the last on 31 July, 2002 (female seen nesting but escaped) (Figure 5). These dates are very similar to those for terrapins nesting at the Jamaica Bay Unit (Feinberg and Burke 2003).

f) The relative amount of terrapins nesting at night vs. nesting in day

Although beaches were raked regularly to detect turtle tracks made after dark, very few indications of night nesting were observed. Only five of the 49 (10%) females captured were encountered after dark.

g) The overall predation rate on SHU terrapin nests

All 39 nests we observed being laid were predated, except for the 11 we successfully protected. Many more nests were laid than we found during oviposition, some of these were not predated. We know that some of the nests we did not discover during oviposition were not predated because we found them post-emergence. Overall, 14 of the 202 nests found were located through the discovery of post-emergence holes. These nests prove that at least some nests avoided predation and produced hatchlings in the absence of wire mesh excluders.

h) Important terrapin predators at SHU

We found ample evidence—tracks, direct observation, usual bite patterns—that demonstrated that raccoons were the primary, and perhaps the only, predators on terrapin nests at SHU. We found no evidence of predation by gulls or foxes. However, foxes would have predated nests without leaving a pile of eggshells right next to the nest cavity.
Raccoons also appeared to have killed seven adult female terrapins. These were found in the nesting areas, laying upside down on the ground or on a piece of wood. Similar predation on adult terrapins has been observed at Jamaica Bay Wildlife Refuge (Feinberg and Burke 2003).

i) Adult terrapins killed by vehicular traffic in 2002

To our knowledge no terrapins were injured or killed by vehicular traffic in 2002, although NPS personnel reported that this has occurred in previous years (Bruce Lane, pers. comm.).

Carcasses from dead terrapins collected and preserved

As described above, seven adult terrapin carcasses were found in summer 2002 at SHU. Of these, five appeared to be fresh kills from 2002 nesting season, two appeared to be older, and may have been killed in 2001 or previous years. These carcasses are being preserved at the Department of Biology, Hofstra University, and will be donated to the specimen collections at the American Museum of Natural History or the National Museum of Natural History. Accession numbers will be sent to NPS when they are available.

j) Hatching success rate for non-predated terrapin nests

Of the 25 nests that avoided predation (11 successfully protected, 14 located post-emergence), 21 produced at least some hatchlings (= 84% nest survivorship). Egg viability (the number of non-predated eggs that hatched) of the protected nests was 71.2% (104/146 eggs). Giambanco (2003) reported egg viability at Jamaica Bay as 88.6%. The relatively low rate at Sandy Hook in 2002 was due to the failure of three nests. Two of these nests, both from the same female, contained 16 and 15 eggs respectively, all of which completely failed to develop. In these nests no embryos were found inside the eggs when they were dissected. Root predation (from dune grass, *Ammophila breviligulata*) predated another nest and resulted in the death of all 11 eggs in the nest. These roots surrounded the eggs, sometimes puncturing them, resulting in non-development of the entire nest.

Of 104 hatched eggs, 94 (90.4%) resulted in hatchlings that emerged from their nests; the remaining hatchlings died after hatching but before emerging. Giambanco (2003) reported similar emergence success at Jamaica Bay at 88.7%.

k) Standard morphological data on as many terrapins as possible

The measurements for 49 hand-captured female terrapins are listed in Table 1. The average plastron length of nesting females at SHU 2001 was 178.1 mm (std. dev. 11.0, range: 151-222, Table 1) very similar to the 172.9 mm reported for nesting females at Jamaica Bay Wildlife Refuge (Feinberg 2000).

l) Uniquely mark as many terrapins as possible as a basis for future studies

Each captured female received a unique identification notch number (Table 1, Figure 3) for future identification.

m) Attach return tags to as many terrapins as possible

Aluminum return tags (Figure 4) were glued onto backs of all captured females. The numbers on the return tags are depicted in Table 1. Two females lost their return tags, therefore they received new return tag numbers when recaptured. These tags will allow future researchers to determine if the turtles leave the Sandy Hook bay.

n) Blood samples for genetic comparison with other GNRA populations

Blood samples were taken from 20 of the captured females. These samples have been added to the large dataset collected by Kristen Hart (Duke University) for a range-wide study of genetic variation in *Malaclemys terrapin*.

Conclusions

Because this study provided only preliminary information on the population count and location of nesting areas, future studies are needed in order to further understand terrapin population trends at SHU. For example, the data collected are insufficient to estimate the population sex ratio, clutch frequency, and nest site fidelity. We found evidence that individual females do nest repeatedly in the same general location. Also, although the nesting sites are not generally accessible to the public, raccoons are able to search out and find these areas. All of the nests we observed being laid were predated by raccoons unless the nests were protected, although some other nests did survive. The highest number of emergence holes was found on the Plum Island, possibly due to the fact that there are people present on the site, which may have disrupted raccoon predation on nests. These high predation rates are potentially dangerous to the persistence of the terrapin population if recruitment is reduced below rates required for population maintenance.

Raccoons not only predated nests, but also killed adult turtles. During 2002 alone at least five adult females were killed. If our estimate of a minimum of 250 adult terrapins in this population is correct, this amounts to a loss of 2.0% per year. This rate of loss may not be sustainable if recruitment is low, as it appears. Predation on nesting females can have a severe impact on survival of populations of typically long-lived species such as turtles, and such predation has been known to drive terrapin populations to extinction in a situation very similar to that at SHU (Seigel 1993).

In the future, wire mesh excluders could be used to protect more nests, at least through the incubation period. Also, the raccoon population could be reduced, which could be justified on the basis that it is unnaturally high due to anthropogenic habitat alteration and food subsidies. Otherwise, it is possible that in the coming decades the terrapin population at Sandy Hook could be greatly reduced or even eliminated as a result of predation on eggs and adults.

Additionally, visitors should be informed on the nesting habits of these turtles, so during the nesting season they would be less likely to approach nesting terrapins and scare the terrapins off of their nests.

Literature Cited

Conant, R., and Collins, J. T. 1998. Reptiles and amphibians of eastern and central North America: Peterson Field Guides. Houghton Mifflin Company, New York.

Feinberg, J. A. 2000. Nesting ecology of the diamondback terrapin (*Malaclemys terrapin*) at Gateway National Recreation Area. Unpublished M.S. thesis, Hofstra University. 116 pp.

Feinberg, J.A. and R.L. Burke. 2003. Nesting ecology and predation of diamondback terrapins, *Malaclemys terrapin*, at Gateway National Recreation Area, New York. Journal of Herpetology 37:517-526.

Giambanco, M. R. 2003. Comparison of viability rates, hatchling survivorship and sex ratios of laboratory and field incubated nests of the estuarine, Emydid turtle *Malaclemys terrapin*. Unpublished M.S. Thesis, Hofstra University, Hempstead, NY.

Hurd, L.E., G.W. Smeds and T.A. Dean. 1979. An ecological study of natural population of diamondback terrapins *Malaclemys terrapin* in Delaware salt marsh. Estuaries 2: 28–33.

Roosenburg, W. M. 1991. The diamondback terrapin: population dynamics, habitat requirements, and opportunities for conservation. In J. A. Mihursky and A. Chaney (eds.), New Perspectives in Chesapeake System: A Research and Management Partnership, pp. 237–244. Research Consortium, Proceeding of a Conference. 4-6 December 1990, Baltimore, MD.

Seigel, R. A. 1993. Recent population changes: apparent long-term decline in diamondback terrapin populations at the Kennedy Space Center, Florida. Herpetological Review 24: 102–103.

NPS D-380 March 2005

National Park Service
U.S. Department of the Interior

Northeast Region
Inventory & Monitoring Program
15 State Street
Boston, Massachusetts 02109

http://www.nps.gov/nero/science/